Football

Great Moments, Records, and Facts

by Teddy Borth

ABDO
GREAT SPORTS
Kids

abdopublishing.com

Published by Abdo Kids, a division of ABDO, PO Box 398166, Minneapolis, Minnesota 55439.

Printed in the United States of America, North Mankato, Minnesota.

102014

012015

THIS BOOK CONTAINS
RECYCLED MATERIALS

Photo Credits: AP Images, Getty Images, Shutterstock, © Aspen Photo / Shutterstock p.5

Production Contributors: Teddy Borth, Jennie Forsberg, Grace Hansen

Design Contributors: Laura Rask, Dorothy Toth

Library of Congress Control Number: 2014943654

Cataloging-in-Publication Data

Borth, Teddy.

 Football : great moments, records, and facts / Teddy Borth.

   p. cm. -- (Great sports)

ISBN 978-1-62970-689-4 (lib. bdg.)

Includes bibliographical references and index.

1. Football--Juvenile literature.   I. Title.

796.332--dc23

                    2014943654

Table of Contents

Football

College teams started playing football in 1869. Each team had its own rules. The game grew. The rules continue to change today.

Football Field

The largest stadiums in the United States are for college teams. They can hold more than 100,000 people!

Great Records

Jerry Rice played in the NFL for 20 seasons. He has the most catches. He has the most **touchdown** catches. He has the most yards of any **receiver**.

9

Brett Favre played in 297 games in a row. He played almost every game for 20 years. No player has ever come close to that number.

Coaches thought Emmitt Smith was too small for the NFL. They were wrong. He holds the most running yards of any player.

One Yard Short

The Rams and Titans are playing in the 2000 **Super Bowl**. The Rams are winning by 7 points. There are six seconds left. Titans have the ball.

McNair passes to Dyson. He runs to the goal. He is caught! Dyson reaches the ball out. He's stopped short of the goal line. The Rams win the **Super Bowl**!

The Catch

The Cowboys and 49ers are playing on January 10, 1982. The winner goes to the **Super Bowl**. The 49ers are losing 21–27. Joe Montana takes his team to the six-yard line.

19

Montana throws the ball high. The ball looks like it will go into the stands. Dwight Clark reaches up. He grabs the ball with his fingertips. **Touchdown**! This play is called "The Catch."

21

More Facts

- The **Super Bowl** is the most watched television program in the United States. About 36 percent of Americans will watch it.

- The average NFL game is 3 hours from start to finish. Of those 3 hours, the ball is only in play for 11 minutes.

- The Pro Bowl started in 1939. The game was played at the end of the season. A team made of the year's best players would play the team who won the league. The all-star team lost the first four games. The Pro Bowl was later changed so both teams were made up of the best players.

Glossary

receiver – a player who catches the football.

Super Bowl – the game to find the number one team in the NFL. It is the last game of the season.

touchdown – a score made when the ball crosses the goal line. A touchdown is worth 6 points with a chance of 1 or 2 extra points after.

23

Index

abdokids.com

Use this code to log on to abdokids.com and access crafts, games, videos and more!

Abdo Kids Code:
GFK6894